Gliding
Across the Gobi

Rob Waring, *Series Editor*

HEINLE
CENGAGE Learning

Australia • Brazil • Japan • Korea • Mexico • Singapore • Spain • United Kingdom • United States

Words to Know

This story is set in an area
of China called Inner Mongolia.
It happens in Badain Jaran
[bɑːdɑːin dʒərɑːn], which
is in the Gobi Desert.

 The Gobi Desert. Read the paragraph. Write the number of the correct word in **bold** next to each item in the picture. Then answer the questions.

The Gobi Desert covers a large part of Inner Mongolia. Deserts are usually covered with **sand** (1). The Badain Jaran area of the Gobi Desert is unusual because it has large **lakes** (2) as well as huge sand dunes. Despite the arid environment, many people live in the Gobi Desert. They usually live in **tents** (3) and often use **camels** (4) for travelling, because camels can survive for a long time without water.

5. Which of these definitions describes a <u>dune</u>?
   a. a mountain of sand
   b. a large piece of land

6. Which of these definitions describes <u>arid</u>?
   a. a hot, dry place
   b. a place in China

The Badain Jaran Area of the Gobi Desert

B Desert Explorers. Look at the picture and read the paragraph. Notice the words in **bold**. Then answer the questions.

This story is about two **explorers**, George Steinmetz [staɪmɛts] and Don Webster. In the story, these explorers go into the Gobi Desert to experience a new adventure. Steinmetz is a **photojournalist** who wants to help people understand the desert better through photographs. To do this, he wants to take photos while he is paragliding. Why? He wants to get a '**bird's eye view**' of the amazing Gobi Desert!

1. What does the word 'explorer' mean? _____

2. What does the word 'photojournalist' mean? _____

3. What does the phrase 'bird's eye view' mean? _____

A man paragliding in the sky.

Far from the rest of the world lies a distant desert land: Badain Jaran. It is **trapped**[1] by some of the world's tallest sand dunes. The Gobi Desert is the fourth largest desert in the world and it's growing larger by hundreds of kilometres every year. For thousands of years the land near the Gobi was very **fertile**,[2] but now it is being threatened. The desert's fast and unstoppable growth may soon change the lives of everyone around it.

---

[1]**trapped:** unable to avoid or escape from a place or situation
[2]**fertile:** possessing a high ability to produce

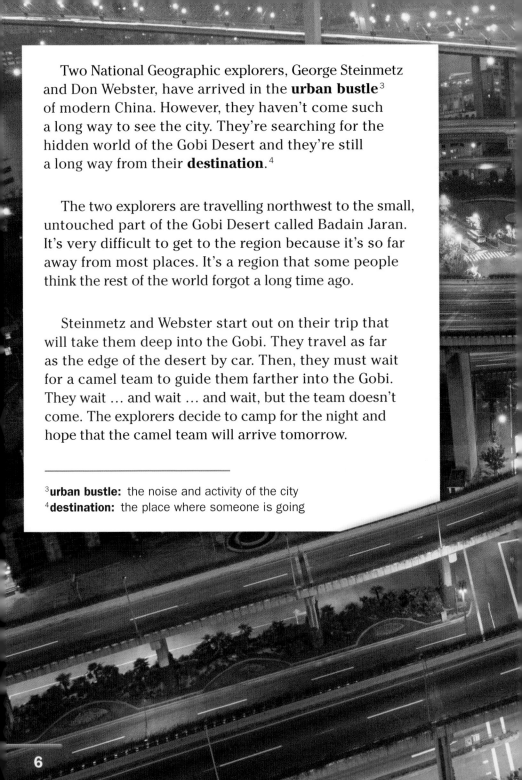

Two National Geographic explorers, George Steinmetz and Don Webster, have arrived in the **urban bustle**[3] of modern China. However, they haven't come such a long way to see the city. They're searching for the hidden world of the Gobi Desert and they're still a long way from their **destination**.[4]

The two explorers are travelling northwest to the small, untouched part of the Gobi Desert called Badain Jaran. It's very difficult to get to the region because it's so far away from most places. It's a region that some people think the rest of the world forgot a long time ago.

Steinmetz and Webster start out on their trip that will take them deep into the Gobi. They travel as far as the edge of the desert by car. Then, they must wait for a camel team to guide them farther into the Gobi. They wait … and wait … and wait, but the team doesn't come. The explorers decide to camp for the night and hope that the camel team will arrive tomorrow.

---

[3]**urban bustle:** the noise and activity of the city
[4]**destination:** the place where someone is going

Predict

Answer the questions using the information you know from reading to this point. Then, scan pages 9 and 11 to check your answers.

1. When will the camel team arrive?

2. How many camels will there be?

3. How hot will it get in the desert?

RUSSIA

KAZ.

MONGOLIA

CHINA Beijing★

•Lanzhou

Plateau DIRECTION
of Tibet OF VIEW

0 mi   500

0 km 500

R U S S I

M O N G O L I A

A L T A Y   M O U N T A

Ejin Qi

C H I N A

Dunhuang *Bei Shan*

A

Badai

De

Yumenguan

Jiayuguan

Altun Shan *Qilian Sh*

Qinghai
Hu

At 1,300,000 square kilometres, the Gobi Desert
is nearly twice the size of the U.S. state of Texas.
It often gets less than three inches of rain a year.
In fact, the word 'Gobi' means 'waterless place'.

Early the next morning, their guide, **Lao Ji**,[5] and his camel team finally arrive. Lao Ji has 22 camels and they know the desert well. He was born and raised in this arid region, so he will be able to take the explorers safely into the centre, or heart, of the desert.

After Lao Ji arrives, the group sits down with a map to carefully plan their **route**[6] into the desert. This is important because the Gobi is huge and it can get very hot. It could be easy to get lost in this dry, empty place. The team needs to work with one another to be sure that they can successfully reach their destination.

------

[5] **Lao Ji:** [laʊ dʒiː]
[6] **route:** the path along which one travels

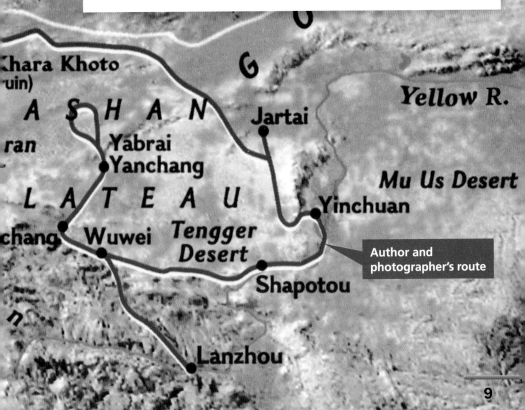

N S

Khara Khoto
(uin)

A S H A N

Jartai

Yellow R.

ran

Yabrai
Yanchang

Mu Us Desert

L A T E A U

Yinchuan

chang

Wuwei

Tengger
Desert

Shapotou

Author and
photographer's route

Lanzhou

The group is now ready to begin their long **trek**[7] deep into the desert. As they start to walk, the dunes slowly rise beside them, and the temperature rises, too. By noon, it reaches **120 degrees Fahrenheit**,[8] and there is nowhere to hide from the heat. Trees rarely grow this far out in the desert, so there is no **shade**[9] from the sun. According to Steinmetz, there would be only two possible situations if someone were to get lost in the Gobi. 'I think getting lost here … it could be bad, or it could be very bad,' he says, smiling slightly at the joke.

Even though it's an easy place to get lost, Steinmetz, a National Geographic photojournalist, actually likes the desert. As he walks along, he takes a break to look around him and says, 'It's beautiful, absolutely beautiful.' He then continues to express his amazement at the size and the beauty of the land, 'It's amazing; this is like … the result of 40 million years of winds.'

---

[7]**trek:** a long difficult journey
[8]**120 degrees Fahrenheit:** 48.89 degrees Celsius
[9]**shade:** slight darkness caused by something blocking the direct light from the sun

As the explorers hike farther into the desert, the conditions become even more extreme. By day three, the dunes are more than **1,000 feet**[10] high and it takes one full day to climb a single sand mountain. It's really hard work.

Steinmetz talks about just how distant this place is from other towns and cities. He says, 'I think this is about as 'inner' as you get in Inner Mongolia; four days by camel through 1,000-foot dunes.' He then continues to describe the feeling of separation from the rest of the world. 'It's so far from anywhere else,' he says. 'I mean, this is the place that time forgot. It's just beautiful.'

---

[10]**1,000 feet:** 304.8 metres

Infer Meaning

1. What does Steinmetz mean by 'as inner as you get in Inner Mongolia'?

2. What does he mean by 'the place that time forgot'?

At last, the explorers reach their planned meeting point in Badain Jaran. Steinmetz is going to meet his friend **Alain Arnoux**[11] here so he and Arnoux can paraglide over the desert dunes. Even though one of the most exciting parts of their adventure is about to begin, the team must first wait for his arrival. In less than an hour, their wait is over. Arnoux finally arrives and makes a fantastic entrance. He flies in to the explorers' camp by paraglider! Steinmetz and Arnoux are very happy to see each other, and welcome each other excitedly. They will have lots of stories to tell this evening!

---

[11]**Alain Arnoux:** [ɑːlẹn ɑːrnuː]

That night, there is a very special dinner in a big tent at the camp. The whole group gathers together to have a good time while they talk, laugh and eat. In Inner Mongolia, having a good time often means eating lots of **mutton**[12] and listening to music. One of the ladies in the group sings traditional songs as the other members enjoy a delicious meal. 'It's nice to have a full tent,' says Steinmetz as he relaxes with his friends.

---

[12]**mutton:** meat from a sheep

After all the wonderful food and drink, it's not easy to get up the next morning. However, Steinmetz and Arnoux wake up very early to prepare themselves for their first paraglide together, and they're very excited about it.

Arnoux is one of the best paragliders in the world, and he has come to help Steinmetz learn how to do it. An adventure like this requires careful planning. First, the two adventurers prepare their equipment and look at a map so they can plan their route. Steinmetz proposes that they fly over a number of different lakes and then return to the starting point. At last, the two paragliders are ready to go.

Steinmetz goes first. He puts on all of his equipment, which includes a safety helmet on his head and a fan-like engine on his back. He then carefully arranges his paraglider sail behind him so that he can pull it with him. Finally, he tries to **take off**.[13] He must speed up the engine and run quickly. At the same time, he must pull the big paraglider sail until it goes up and catches the wind.

Unfortunately, Steinmetz just can't get off the ground. What's wrong? As Arnoux runs to see what the problem is, he explains, 'His engine … it maybe doesn't work well.' When he reaches Steinmetz, the tired paraglider explains that he just can't get enough power. The two men try again and again. The good morning sunlight is going fast, and the wind conditions have become difficult. Steinmetz still can't get enough speed to take off!

---

[13]**take off:** leave the ground; start flying

paraglider sail

helmet

engine

Steinmetz tries to take off for the first time, but he can't get enough speed.

The two men keep trying to get Steinmetz up in the air, but both are beginning to get tired. Then, finally and after many failed attempts, Steinmetz manages to get off the ground. At last he takes off and rises high into the air. Arnoux quickly follows and the other members of the group watch the two men as they fly through the air. The sport of paragliding looks very exciting from the ground. The two men **glide**[14] smoothly over the desert using their engines to help keep them in the air. 'Oh, he's having a good time,' says National Geographic writer Don Webster as he watches Steinmetz fly off.

---

[14]**glide:** move smoothly and quietly

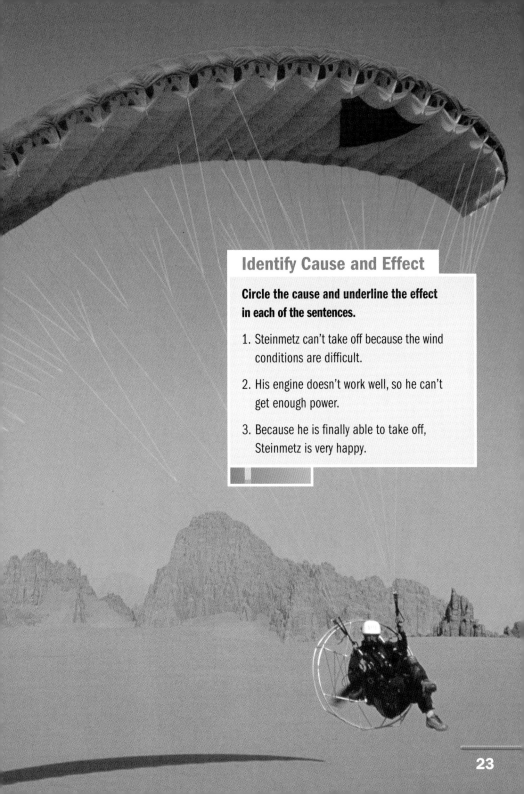

Identify Cause and Effect

Circle the cause and underline the effect in each of the sentences.

1. Steinmetz can't take off because the wind conditions are difficult.

2. His engine doesn't work well, so he can't get enough power.

3. Because he is finally able to take off, Steinmetz is very happy.

Steinmetz can finally do what he really wants to do – take photos of Badain Jaran from high above. He can get photos that are from a bird's eye view. Steinmetz explains why he wants to take these pictures, 'The picture … the view I really want, is being able to really understand what makes this place so **unique**.'[15] He adds, 'There's no other place in the world that has this size of dune – and with lakes in between. It's the most beautiful place in the world to me.' Steinmetz needs to be high in the sky to be able to photograph the desert's many features.

From above, the photojournalist can also see how small people seem when they are compared with the desert. He says that it's difficult to believe that people can actually live in it. The view also reminds him of another fact that's not so pleasant. It reminds him that the growing desert may soon completely change the lives of everyone around it.

---

[15]**unique:** special and different

After his first trip, Steinmetz returns to the take off area safely, but then goes up once more. He wants to take one last picture. In his photographs, he really wants to demonstrate the relationship between the desert and its people. For him, flying above the Gobi makes him feel closer to the desert itself. It also helps him to better understand the people who live there. For Steinmetz, gliding across the Gobi has been an experience he won't soon forget.

After You Read

1. Which of the following explains why Badain Jaran is in danger?
   A. Explorers are coming.
   B. The people are changing.
   C. It's a long way from the rest of China.
   D. The desert is growing.

2. The explorers are travelling to the Gobi by:
   A. paragliding
   B. car
   C. camel
   D. train

3. The Gobi Desert is _____ to find and _____ away.
   A. far, travel
   B. hard, far
   C. easy, hidden
   D. long, hidden

4. The writer thinks that Lao Ji is a good guide because he has a camel team.
   A. True
   B. False

5. On page 11, why does the writer say 'there is nowhere to hide'?
   A. The dunes are too big.
   B. The temperature is 130 degrees.
   C. There is no cool place.
   D. 11 a.m. is the hottest time.

6. How high are the dunes in the Gobi Desert?
   A. about 2,000 feet
   B. about 300 metres
   C. about 1,000 metres
   D. about 300 feet

7. On page 19, 'it' refers to:
   A. taking off
   B. planning their visit
   C. becoming the best
   D. paragliding

8. Which is the best heading for page 25?
   A. Flying Next to the Dunes
   B. A View from Above
   C. Paragliding Writer
   D. The Beautiful Lakes

9. George thinks that people find it difficult to live in the Gobi.
   A. True
   B. False

10. On page 26, in the phrase 'feel closer', 'closer' can be replaced by:
   A. connected to
   B. nearby
   C. better
   D. happier

11. While paragliding over the Gobi, George sees _____ scene he will never forget.
   A. some
   B. a
   C. only
   D. lots of

12. The writer probably thinks that George's experience is:
   A. appealing
   B. scary
   C. mysterious
   D. complicated

An Introduction to Desert Ecology

A desert is defined as a place that gets less than 250 millimetres (mm) of rain each year. It differs sharply from the climate of a rain forest, which can receive up to 10,000 mm of rain annually. The charts here demonstrate this difference. Arid desert lands cover about one third of the earth's surface. Most deserts are covered with sand, which is often in the form of hills called sand dunes. There are also usually a lot of rocky areas. This combination of sand and rock means that the soil is not very fertile.

Even though the desert environment is very dry and hot, some living things are able to do well in this setting. Many plants and animals have changed and developed in ways that help them to live in the desert. These changes have become apparent in a number of ways. Some plants are able to grow very quickly whenever it rains. They turn green and produce flowers within just a few days. Other plants grow farther underground to find water as far as 25 metres away. Some desert plants simply stop growing in very dry weather. They appear to be dead, but when the rain returns, they come back to life and begin growing again.

Desert animals have also developed many characteristics that help them to survive in an arid environment. Camels are an excellent example of this. These strange-looking animals need very little water in hot, dry conditions. This allows them to go for a very long time without drinking. Some birds avoid the heat by flying out of the desert during the hottest

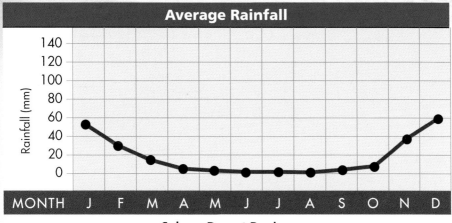

Sahara Desert Region

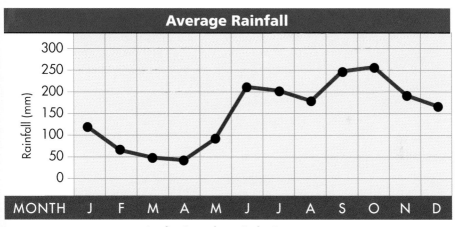

Latin American Rain Forest

part of the year. Other animals, such as snakes and rats, find cool places to sleep during the day and come out only at night. The extremely long ears of desert rabbits help them to better distribute their body heat and stay cool. Changes like these have allowed some animals and plants to grow and develop successfully in a very challenging ecological system: the desert.

Word Count: 332
Time: _____

Vocabulary List

arid (2, 9)
bird's eye view (3, 25)
camel (2, 6, 7, 9, 12)
destination (6, 9)
dune (2, 4, 11, 12, 15, 25)
explorer (3, 6, 9, 12, 15)
fertile (4)
lake (2, 19, 25, 26)
glide (22, 26)
mutton (17)
photojournalist (3, 11, 25)
route (9, 19)
sand (2, 4, 12)
shade (11)
take off (20, 21, 22, 23, 26)
tent (2, 17)
trapped (4)
trek (11)
unique (25)
urban bustle (6)